The Zoo's
Who's Who

Kangaroos

Katie Franks

PowerKiDS
press

New York

Published in 2015 by The Rosen Publishing Group, Inc.
29 East 21st Street, New York, NY 10010

First Edition

Editor: Jennifer Way
Photo Research: Katie Stryker
Book Design: Joe Carney

Photo Credits: Cover Volodymyr/Shutterstock.com; pp. 5, 9, 17, 18, 22 iStock/Thinkstock; p. 6 Mint Images - Frans Lanting/Getty Images; p. 10 Danita Delimont/Gallo Images/Getty Images; p. 13 worldswildlifewonders/ Shutterstock.com; p. 14 Robyn Butler/Shutterstock.com; p. 21 Anna Jurkovska/Shutterstock.com; p. 24 Tim Phillips Photos/Flickr/Getty Images.

Library of Congress Cataloging-in-Publication Data

Franks, Katie.
Kangaroos / by Katie Franks.
    pages cm. — (The zoo's who's who)
Includes index.
ISBN 978-1-4777-6471-8 (library binding) — ISBN 978-1-4777-6572-2 (pbk.) —
ISBN 978-1-4777-6573-9 (6-pack)
1. Kangaroos—Juvenile literature. I. Title.
QL737.M35F67 2015
599.2'22—dc23
                                        2013047733

Manufactured in the United States of America

CPSIA Compliance Information: Batch #WS14PK4: For Further Information contact Rosen Publishing, New York, New York at 1-800-237-9932

Contents

Kangaroos are a family of animals that live in Australia. There are two kinds of gray kangaroos.

The red kangaroo is the largest kangaroo. This kind of kangaroo lives in **deserts** and grasslands.

Kangaroos are plant eaters.
They eat mostly grasses.

Kangaroos move by jumping. Their strong tails help them **balance**.

Kangaroos can move 30 feet (9 m) in one hop. Kangaroos can also swim!

A group of kangaroos is a mob.
A mob lives and travels together.

A mother kangaroo carries her baby in her **pouch**. Baby kangaroos are called joeys.

Kangaroos sniff other members of the mob. They do this as a **greeting**.

Male kangaroos fight over female kangaroos. They push and hit with their front legs. They kick with their back legs.

21

22

Kangaroos live in zoos all over the world.

WORDS TO KNOW

balance   **deserts**   **greeting**   **pouch**

WEBSITES

Due to the changing nature of Internet links, PowerKids Press has developed an online list of websites related to the subject of this book. This site is updated regularly. Please use this link to access the list:
www.powerkidslinks.com/zww/kang/

INDEX

24